LAWRENCE OF ARABIA

Text by
DAVID NICOLLE PhD
Colour plates by
RICHARD HOOK

First published in Great Britain in 1989 by
Osprey Publishing, Elms Court, Chapel Way,
Botley, Oxford OX2 9LP, United Kingdom.
Email: info@ospreypublishing.com

Also published as Men-at-Arms 208 *Lawrence and the Arab Revolts*

ISBN 1 84176 114 1

Filmset in Great Britain
Printed in China through World Print Ltd.

FOR A CATALOGUE OF ALL BOOKS PUBLISHED BY
OSPREY MILITARY, AUTOMOTIVE AND AVIATION
PLEASE WRITE TO:

The Marketing Manager, Osprey Direct USA,
PO Box 130, Sterling Heights, MI 48311-0130, USA.
Email: info@ospreydirectusa.com

The Marketing Manager, Osprey Direct UK,
PO Box 140, Wellingborough, Northants, NN8 4ZA,
United Kingdom.
Email: info@ospreydirect.co.uk

VISIT OSPREY AT
www.ospreypublishing.com

Dedication

That my friends may yet be free.

Errata

The figure Plate G1 should have a dark green waist
sash showing beneath his belt equipment.

FRONT and BACK COVERS: T.E. Lawrence
(Imperial War Museum)

Lawrence of Arabia

Introduction

The Great War of 1914–1918 is often seen as one major battleground—the Western Front—with numerous 'side-shows'. The other battle zones were not side-shows to those involved, however, although the local inhabitants often fought for motives which remained a closed book to their European allies or foes. Many Middle Eastern combatants saw themselves as defending Islam from Christian domination, for only recently had concepts of nationalism spread beyond the great cities. Only in the Arab Revolt, instigated by the Sharif of Mecca in the Hijaz province of Arabia, was a specifically Arab identity involved, and even here tribal and dynastic motives also played their part.

Even today most Western observers, baffled by such complexities, tend to focus on the activities of a few colourful Europeans caught up in these confusing events, the best known being, of course, T. E. Lawrence—'Lawrence of Arabia'. Numerous books still present him as the leader and inspiration of the Arab Revolt, while what one might call Third World writers often reduce him to a comic irrelevance—or even a Zionist agent. Even a military scholar like Brig. Syed Ali El-Edroos lampoons Lawrence as the 'self-proclaimed genius of the Arab Revolt', and his writings as a 'much publicized but bowdlerised unreliable account of his alleged rôle'. Perhaps the truth lies, as usual, somewhere between. Meanwhile men like Gen.

Arab (Syrian or Iraqi) infantry of the Ottoman Army in 1914.

3

Laperrine, founder of France's camel-mounted Arab Saharan troops, or the German Dr. Wassmuss, whose activities in Iran earned him the title of 'the German Lawrence', remain largely unknown outside their own countries.

While Western Europe has largely digested the appalling upheavals of the Great War, many of those conflicts which still disturb the Middle East either stem from the aftermath of the Great War or, being older in origin, had flared up among that war's 'side-shows'. Such scattered episodes were also what made a singularly savage European civil war into the world's first truly global conflict.

Arabs in the Ottoman Army

French colonial troops of North African origin were thrown into the Western Front fighting within the first few weeks of the Great War, yet the war only really came to the Arab peoples after the Ottoman Empire was drawn in at the end of October 1914. Anatolian Turks naturally formed the core of the Ottoman Army, but minority peoples were also enlisted in great numbers. Arabs were the largest such group and dominated half the Empire's territory, so that in 1914 almost one-third of Ottoman units consisted of Arabs, mostly concentrated in the Arab provinces. A high proportion of their officers were also of Arab origin.

Even before the Ottomans sent their Syrian divisions against the Suez Canal they were also encouraging the bedouin of Sinai to raid British and Egyptian positions. On 30 November 1914 an Ottoman major with 1,500 Syrian bedouin irregulars occupied al Arish and by the end of the year much of Sinai had been overrun. When the Ottoman Army made its thrust against the Suez Canal early in 1915 it did so with a force of only 20,000 men, including two companies of the largely Arab Ottoman Camel Corps under Sami Bey. Though in many ways a desperate gamble, this Ottoman assault across the virtually waterless Sinai desert was a masterpiece of logistics. The attack itself was, however, a dismal failure, partly because of a lack of enthusiasm on the part of the Arab troops. The Ottomans attempted another advance in the spring of 1916 during which the Camel Corps performed very well, capturing a substantial part of a British cavalry regiment at the outposts of Qatiya and Ughratina on 23 April. In fact a number of troops who later fought as Britain's allies in the Arab Revolt had previously fought against the British in Sinai.

Most of the Ottoman troops stationed in Iraq at the start of the war were also Arab, as was at least half the force which attempted to retake Basra from the British in April 1915. Generally speaking they fought for their Ottoman overlords with less determination than did the Syrians, but were subsequently regarded as the best regulars in the ranks of the Sharifian Army (see below). In Gallipoli, however, the largely Arab 8th, 10th and 25th Divisions fought with the same determination as their Turkish comrades. Two Syrian divisions were sent to face the Russians in eastern Anatolia and the British in Iraq. Away to the south in Yemen the Ottoman 7th Corps also consisted largely of Syrian Arabs. After the outbreak of the Arab Revolt in 1916, many Arab troops continued to fight in Ottoman ranks, and even as late as 1918 around a quarter of the Ottoman Army in Syria was of Arab extraction. More reliable, however, were small units of Circassian volunteer cavalry. These were recruited from a local community descended from refugees who had fled the Russian conquest of the Caucasus. Along the northern side of the Yarmuk

Ottoman cavalry encamped near Gaza in April 1917. Note the Arab *kafiya* headcloths which were also used by non-Arab troops (Bundesarchiv).

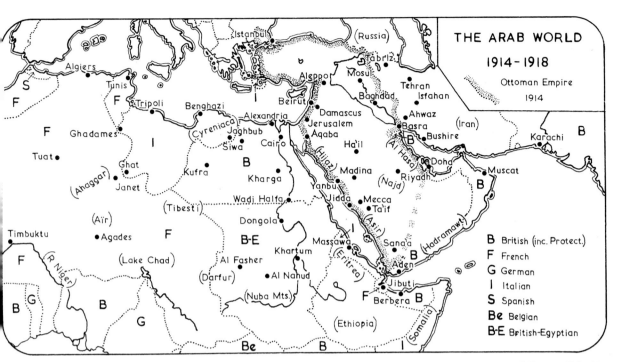

B British (inc. Protect.)
F French
G German
I Italian
S Spanish
Be Belgian
B-E British-Egyptian

River another minority community descended from Algerian refugees adopted a more equivocal position. Though Arab, they were similarly isolated by dialect and culture and, being descended from people driven from North Africa by the French, they fought against further European invasion until the last weeks of the war. More remarkable was the presence of Armenian officers and men among Ottoman troops in Syria as late as 1918 but, not surprisingly, they deserted to the Arab forces whenever an opportunity arose.

The Sanussi and the Sahara

The Sanussi were neither a people nor a sect. Their *tariqa* or 'way' was a reformist movement strictly within Orthodox Islamic principles. Nor at first did they have a political or military structure. Only as a result of encroachment by France and Italy did the Sanussi become anything more than a spiritual movement. Their *zawiyas* or 'lodges' soon became the focus of resistance so that, for a while, foreign invasion actually increased Sanussi influence deep in the desert and the sub-Saharan regions of what became French Sudan.

Nevertheless, by 1914 virtually the entire region had fallen to France and Italy. Only in central Cyrenaica, in what is now eastern Libya, did the Sanussi hold sway. Here their *zawiyas* still served as centres of political, cultural and military resistance, with Kufra as the main Sanussi administrative base. Most *zawiyas* were set in oases, on trading crossroads, near wells or along the Mediterranean coast. Typically they consisted of a warren of narrow lanes, courtyards, mud-brick houses, a mosque, schoolrooms, a barrack-like area for the *ikhwan*—initiates or 'brothers'—and storerooms for food and weapons. Most were surrounded by a simple defensible wall. Even as early as 1890 Jaghbub contained 400 rifles, 200 swords, four small Egyptian cannon, perhaps a gunpowder factory, and some 3,000 men. On Fridays religious students had to do military training which included horsemanship and, rather surprisingly, archery. The surrounding oases were also well tended, as the Sanussi laid great emphasis on agriculture and a settled life.

Until regular forces were established under Ottoman guidance, the Sanussi relied on tribal warriors, and to a large extent continued to do so during the Great War. Tribal warfare had many common features throughout the Arab world, yet these Libyan and Egyptian bedouin also had their own particular traditions. One of the strangest was that of 'Emptying Gunpowder' for any girl who caught a warrior's eye. 'Your face, your face!' the

5

Kurdish irregulars, possibly of the Milli tribe, mobilised to face the Russian invasion of eastern Turkey.

man would cry; and if the lady drew aside her veil she might be honoured by the warrior dancing towards her before firing his gun into the ground within a hair's breadth of her feet. It was, in fact, a matter of pride for a desert maiden to wear singed shoes.

The Italian invasion of Libya

During the long and bitterly contested Italian invasion of Libya, Ottoman officers and NCOs completely reorganised Sanussi forces. There were neither time nor facilities to raise a proper regular army, so bedouin volunteers were formed into guerrilla bands known as *adwar* of between 100 and 300 men. Each had a military commander supported by a few Ottoman advisors, a civil governor or *qaimaqam*, a quartermaster, and a *qadi* or religious judge. This structure survived until the 1920s. Not until their urge to charge the enemy on horseback, armed only with old single-shot guns of Greek manufacture, led to horrendous casualties did these bedouin guerrillas accept Ottoman tactical advice. Meanwhile some 300 young men from leading families were trained as NCOs, armed with Turkish or captured Italian weapons, uniformed and paid as Ottoman regulars. They were then put in charge of the irregulars. Later 365 youngsters were sent for military training in Istanbul; but only 30 returned before the outbreak of the Great War, most of the rest remaining in Turkey, and even fighting against Greek invaders in the 1920s.

Faced with such grim resistance the Italian Army had to rely on modern weaponry, thus becoming the first to use not only aerial bombing but also armoured cars to any great extent. Telegraph lines proved to be even more vital in the vast spaces of Libya, where the Italian Army also developed new tactics based on small mobile forces and numerous locally recruited troops. By 1914 most Sanussi centres had been occupied, and the Italians prepared a major offensive against the remaining Sanussi camps. Only in the old Sanussi heartland of Cyrenaica did they make little progress; here, despite drought, disease, locust plagues and widespread starvation, the Sanussi fought on, helped in secret by Egyptian sympathisers and the Ottoman Empire itself.

As Europe stood on the brink of the Great War it looked as if Italy had finally won its war in Libya; yet it was not to be. Even before the lights went out across Europe, the Italian Army suffered a major reverse when, on 26 August 1914, a large supply column was trapped and virtually wiped out. There were now risings throughout the country while the outbreak of the Great War healed a rift between Sanussi and Turk even before Italy itself declared war on the Ottoman Empire. A major Italian counter-offensive proved a disaster, with 3,500 Libyan auxiliaries going over to the enemy, while thousands more rifles and other supplies fell into Sanussi hands. For the first time in modern history the desert peoples found themselves well armed and, more importantly, with an abundance of ammunition.

The Sanussi invasion of Egypt

The Sanussi had turned the tables; but then, by invading British-occupied Egypt, they again brought military disaster upon themselves. The reasons why the Sanussi took this fateful gamble are still unclear, though hunger and the lure of Egyptian grain probably played a part. In overall command of Sanussi operations was Nuri Pasha, a Turkish Ottoman officer and half-brother of the Young Turk political and military leader Enver Pasha. The Sanussi force which invaded Egypt was also much more formidable than previous Sanussi armies, largely due to the efforts of newly arrived Ottoman advisors. A regular force consisted of seven *Muhafizia* battalions (2,500–3,500 regulars).

Three served with Ja'afar at the front, another was thrust forward to attack enemy communications along the coastal road, and three were held back under Nuri Pasha as a reserve. They were accompanied by perhaps nine 10-pdr. mountain guns and 12 machine-guns; and supported by several thousand bedouin auxiliaries, including camel-mounted infantry and cavalry. Most *Muhafizia* regulars were also recruited from the Ibaidat and Bar'assa tribes of Cyrenaica, while others were drawn from the ranks of Sanussi *ikhawan* initiates. Their discipline, fire-control, and ability to hold entrenched positions and carry out professional tactical manoeuvres added to the effectiveness of their native fighting tradition and set them apart from previous Sanussi armies. Most credit for such developments went to the Ottoman–Iraqi Gen. Ja'afar al Askari, who was later to play a similar rôle moulding the men of the Arab Revolt. The bulk of those who invaded Egypt in November 1915 were,

however, still bedouin tribesmen; and Ja'afar al Askari also proved to be a skilful leader of such untrained hordes.

Ottoman officer and NCO advisors retained their usual uniforms, while the *Muhafizia* wore khaki battledress. Often, however, all troops adopted loose North African costume more suited to desert conditions. Sanussi leaders wore traditional dress and this could sometimes by very rich. One description mentions a yellow and gold *jubbah*, a white silk *kafiya* Arab headdress with a green and gold *agal* around it. Another refers to a yellow silk *kaftan* embroidered with red braid under a white silk *burnus* and the typical white gauze turban of the Sanussi family. These men were religious reformers and, in some respects, puritans, but they were not ascetics.

The bedouin population of Egypt's Western Desert was certainly disaffected in 1915, and there was considerable sympathy for the Sanussi in sections of the Egyptian military. In the event part of the largely settled Awlad 'Ali tribal confederation

...toman auxiliaries of apparent Syrian origin in Palestine ...Bundesarchiv).

Sanussi troops being charged by the Dorset Yeomanry at Aqqaqia, 26 Feb. 1916, from a painting by Lady Butler (Dorset County Council).

went over to the Sanussi; but they were a poor and unwarlike people whose value seems to have been minimal, except for cutting the coastal telegraph wires. Those who did take military action were mostly armed with flintlock muskets whose distinctive 'plop' sound was a feature of many skirmishes. Despite their small numbers the Sanussi proved to be a big problem, tying down far larger numbers of troops until the evacuation of Gallipoli released enough British units for a counter-offensive. Once this began the result was rarely in doubt, however, the main confrontation coming at Aqqaqir in February 1916.

Here the Sanussi held a ridge of sand dunes which provided defensive positions in depth. Machine guns were sited ahead of the main position, but a great many of the irregulars were still armed with single-shot breech-loading rifles whose use of black powder gave the British artillery admirable targets. Sanussi tactics were, as usual, intended to force an attacker to advance under heavy fire; then, using their superior mobility, the Sanussi infantry would withdraw to another position which the British

would again be obliged to attack. The British, however, not only had heavier fire-power but also numerous cavalry and six armoured cars. As the Sanussi withdrew, with baggage camels in front escorted by irregulars and *Muhafizia* guarding the rear and flanks, the Dorset Yeomanry made their famous charge, breaking the Sanussi formations and capturing the wounded Ja'afar Pasha.

Against British armoured cars the Sanussi found no defence; such mechanised assets gave their enemies almost as much freedom of movement as the Arabs themselves enjoyed. Mechanised warfare also drove the Sanussi out of a string of oases deep in the Western Desert, in what is now known as the New Valley. A 350km long narrow-gauge railway was laid from the Nile to Bahariya oasis, defended by a row of fortified blockhouses—all to capture a string of tiny green dots on the face of the desert, defended by no more than 2,000 Sanussi irregulars.

Peace talks between the British, Italians and Sanussi started as early as July 1916, but from the Ottomans' point of view their support of the Sanussi had already achieved remarkable results. By sending no more than 300 soldiers to North Africa with a relatively small amount of munitions and gold they had tied down some 35,000 British and Imperial, about 15,000 French, and at times no less than 60,000 Italian troops in what was probably the most successful covert action of the Great War.

Italy faced serious problems in Libya even before entering the war in 1915. Thereafter Italian military resources were stretched to breaking point. She could do little more than control a few coastal toe-holds and maintain various isolated outposts by heavily defended convoys while the surrounding tribes continued to give the Sanussi information and occasional military support. The majority of strictly Italian troops had been withdrawn to face the Austro-Hungarians, and colonial troops from Eritrea now proved to be the most loyal and effective forces available in Libya. Nevertheless Italian troops, including five-ton Bianchi armoured cars, did take part in mopping-up operations as the British drove Sanussi forces back across the Egyptian frontier. In addition to armoured cars the Italians made considerable use of aircraft, including the latest three-engined Caproni bombers, whose 1000lb bomb load was an extraordinary compliment to the military tenacity of the poorly armed

Sanussi and their allies. Naval firepower was also widely used to support coastal garrisons.

The struggle in Libya did not, however, end when the Sanussi, British and Italians signed their peace accords at Akrama in April 1917, though they did lead to an armed truce which persisted right up until the third and final Italo–Sanussi War of 1922. It left the Italian garrisons surrounded by Sanussi forces which the Italian government had also agreed to supply with uniforms, 2,000 additional rifles, another battery of mountain artillery and substantial amounts of money. For their part the Sanussi agreed to help against a non-Sanussi resistance movement in Tripolitania, led by Ramadan al Shtaiwi and the Ottoman Nuri Pasha. A briefly independent republic was declared in 1918. Resistance also continued in the Fezzan, deep in the south-western desert of Libya. Peace with the Sanussi had, however, freed the Italian Army to concentrate upon these other centres of opposition, which it did after the end of the Great War in Europe, with crushing success.

The Tuareg and the Sahara

Although the French invasion of the Sahara led to a brief expansion of Sanussi power, by 1914 the French advance had confined Sanussi influence roughly within what is today Libya. But, following a series of Italian defeats by the Sanussi in 1914–15, the French found themselves facing not only serious

Bedouin chiefs under interrogation at Mersa Matruh, early 1916 (IWM).

The mud-brick citadel of Siwa oasis, a major Sanussi centre before its destruction (IWM).

unrest but open warfare with the Sanussi. Unlike the British, who had greater reserves of Imperial troops, the French had to rely on local forces. Many colonial troops had already been sent to face the German assault, and of those that remained the most important were the camel-mounted Saharan infantry recruited almost entirely from Arab Shaamba bedouin. Gen. Laperrine had turned them into an effective force; but this gifted officer, along with many of his colleagues, had been recalled to the Western Front. In fact at the end of 1914 there were only three companies of *méhariste* camel troops left to control the vast Tuat, Saura and Tidikelt regions. Some local irregular forces, known as *goums*, were also recruited while in late 1915–early 1916 new *saharienne* companies were formed to patrol the similarly extensive Uwargla and Tuggurt regions.

The defence of the entire Sahara seemed to depend on tiny far-flung outposts supplied by vulnerable camel caravans. Some protection was given by the Great Eastern Erg sand sea, but even this did not prevent daring raids by dissident Shaamba, Tuareg and Jiramma tribesmen supported by Sanussi forces based at Ghadames across the Libyan frontier. French morale slumped following a string of military reverses in which a number of French officers and NCOs fell into Sanussi hands.

Salih al Baskari, the Sanussi governor of Kufra, with a senior officer of the Sanussi Army photographed shortly after the Great War (Royal Geographical Society).

Tuareg drum-groups who refused to make peace with the French had already migrated to Ghat and Ghadames in Libya, where they joined forces with the Sanussi to take revenge against the European invader. Fortunately for the French the Tuareg tribes or drum-groups could never unify. Even the symbolic authority of a regional *amenoukal* or leader was only agreed after endless discussion, and there were three main drum-groups in the mountainous Ahaggar region of the central Sahara alone. While the Arab tribes had always been better armed than their Berber-speaking Tuareg rivals, the Tuareg themselves were now getting captured Italian rifles. By 1914 Tuareg military and social structure was also changing. Traditionally only the nobility owned the camels vital to movement in the deep desert, and only they could wear the double-edged *takouba* swords which symbolised their status. The vassals traditionally took no part in war; but since the turn of the century some nobles had armed their vassals, who thus became warriors in their own right, increasingly claiming a political voice and probably dominating warfare as they outnumbered

the old nobility by eight to one. Traditional Tuareg tactics had despised firearms, because they possessed so few, and instead spears were hurled from camel-back before hand-to-hand combat with swords. By 1914, however, they had developed considerable skill in skirmishing with their newly acquired rifles.

Many Tibu tribesmen also turned against the French during the Great War, but they were even more poorly armed than the Tuareg. Even as late as the 1920s this nomadic Sudanese people were described as dressed in skins and taking such care of their few cotton clothes that they would remove their trousers while riding to avoid wear and tear. On one occasion a Tibu was prepared to retrace an entire day's march across the desert because he thought he had dropped them on the way, his Arab companions having hidden his trousers as a joke. The majority of Arab Shaamba tribesmen remained loyal to France, though some rallied to the Sanussi and, with their better weapons and discipline, were probably of greater military value than the Tibu and Tuareg combined.

The first Sanussi attacks on French territory consisted of minor raids but on 16 March 1916 a *harka* or war-band of several hundred men attacked the French outpost at Janet. This force had been assembled at Ghat and had plenty of modern rifles plus a few machine guns, cannon and Ottoman advisers. After nine days the French garrison attempted to break out but were soon captured, the French prisoners being taken to Waw al Kabir. There, in a tiny oasis in the far south-east of Libya, they and other French prisoners remained until the end of the war. This Sanussi success prompted risings over a huge area; but, surprisingly perhaps, the Tuareg of the Ahaggar mountains followed the cautious advice of their *amenoukal*, Musa ag Aamastane, and kept the Sanussi at arm's length. Not so the southern Ullimende Tuareg of the Aïr region in what is now Niger. Their *amenoukal*, Firhun, escaped from French custody and, with some 1,500 tribesmen, attacked the outpost of Manaka. This attack was, however, driven off and on 9 May 1916 Firhun's men were defeated by a combined force of French troops and Ahaggar Tuareg.

December 1916 was the worst time for French forces in the Sahara with various outposts falling and even the town of Agades being placed under siege. Casualties rose and more French officers fell into Sanussi hands, the most senior being Brig. Béchet who was captured along with an entire supply caravan just south of the Great Eastern Erg sand sea. Such a prisoner was potentially very valuable to Ahmad Zirrug, the Sanussi *qaimaqam* of Ghadames. Zirrug was a black ex-serf from Ghat who had risen through the ranks of the Sanussi army until he commanded 100 camel-mounted infantry. But his people were now suffering terrible hunger following droughts and locust swarms. Zirrug hoped to trade Béchet for supplies, but the involvement of British and Italian negotiators complicated the issue. Nothing was done, the famine that gripped the Sahara grew worse, all food ran out, and a 35 day famine began in the Fezzan area where the prisoners were held. Local people and refugees died at a rate of five to ten per day. Béchet himself succumbed on 6 July 1918 and only one Frenchman, Sous-Officier Lapierre, remained alive when a Sanussi emissary arrived with orders to release all prisoners.

By then, of course, the war in the Sahara had run its course. Gen. Laperrine had been recalled from the Western Front, a new military command structure at last covered the entire Saharan war-zone, and defensive strategy was replaced by aggressive patrolling. The siege of Agades was lifted. The southern Ilamane Tuareg were defeated in battle on 5 April 1917; loyal tribes were rewarded while others were won over. Sanussi forces along the Niger River were dispersed and had to abandon large-scale operations with artillery. Raiding and guerrilla action continued, but by January 1918 the rebellion had collapsed, the French Sahara remaining relatively quiet until 1956.

'Ali Dinar of Darfur

Even while the British, French and Italians were struggling to cope with the widespread effects of Sanussi activity another crisis was brewing further south. The Sultanate of Darfur ('Land of the Fur') lay within the Anglo–Egyptian Sudan but was not administered as part of that shared domain. The Fur were Muslim Sudanese but a few other tribes within Darfur spoke Arabic. West of the dry rugged hills of Darfur lay the French-ruled plains of Wadai and Lake Chad, while to the east stretched the open spaces of Khordofan and the fertile upper Nile.

Following the defeat of the Mahdist revolt in 1899, a leader of the Tama tribe named 'Ali Dinar was set up as British Agent for Darfur. His army

Soldiers of the Sanussi Army seen shortly after the Great War (Royal Geographical Society).

was, however, defeated by the supposedly subordinate Rizaiqat tribe in 1913, and 'Ali Dinar went on to quarrel with most of his neighbours. 'Ali Dinar had also made contact with the Sanussi of Kufra, and when the Ottoman Empire entered the war he was the only major Sudanese leader not to send a message of support to the Anglo–Egyptian authorities. Not surprisingly Khartoum now viewed 'Ali Dinar with suspicion. He was no mere tribal bandit: 'Ali Dinar's palace at al Fasher was described as a miniature Alhambra, and his army was a formidable force by African standards.

Before its costly defeat by the Rizaiqat the Darfur army consisted of about 6,000 riflemen and 1,700 cavalry. An élite formed the Sultan's *malazimin* or bodyguard, the rest being divided into three *arba'* (sing. *ruba'*) divisions, each being an independent tactical unit of regular infantry and cavalry. To this army were attached irregulars organised on a territorial basis. Even the regulars received no pay, although they did get occasional gifts of cattle or sheep. Theoretically each *ruba'* was subdivided into *miya* of 100 men under a *ras miya*. By 1916, however, the army had shrunk to no more than 5,000 men divided into a larger number of *arba'*, while the *miyas* of even the Sultan's guard were down to 60 or so men, those of the ordinary army being as low as 30. Most were based in al Fasher where, in addition to

Tuareg nobles of the Ahaggar mountains of southern Algeria shortly before the Great War (Royal Geographical Society).

some 800 regular cavalry, there were 3,000 regula[r] infantry with rifles but poor training and in[-]adequate ammunition, and up to 2,000 spear[-]armed irregulars.

Although firearms were abundant they wer[e] mostly old-fashioned large-bore Carambil rifle[s] imported from Egypt or North Africa, plus a fe[w] Remingtons or Martinis, archaic muzzle-loadin[g] muskets and even double-barrelled shotguns. Eac[h] man was generally issued with no more than fiv[e] rounds even on campaign. A small munition[s] factory produced 2,000–3,000 rounds per year[,] while 'Ali Dinar's artillery was limited to a couple o[f] small, ex-Egyptian cannon. In December 1915 th[e] Sultan claimed to have recieved 2,500 Mauser rifle[s] and 400 cases of ammunition from the Sanussi[,] though in reality he appears to have got only 26[0] rifles and two boxes of cartridges. Other traditiona[l] Fur weapons included the peculiar *safariq*, a heav[y] wooden axe-like device, curved and straigh[t] daggers, all-iron multi-spiked throwing axes; an[d] straight-bladed *kaskara* swords similar to the Tuare[g] *takouba*. (The idea that such swords were in some way influenced by European 'Crusader' swords is of course, nonsense.) The Fur army had n[o] uniforms although all wore typical knee-lengt[h] Sudanese *jubbahs*, those of senior men being of fine[r] cotton or silk.

Despite this weakened army, 'Ali Dinar became increasingly defiant, refused to accept Britain'[s] deposition of the Egyptian Khedive Abbas II in 1914, and corresponded with the Sanussi in Libya. He sent a letter to the Ottoman Sultan claiming that his Rizaiqat tribal rivals had been destroyed by a rain of heavenly fire and another to Khartoum[,] addressed to 'The Governor of Hell in Kordofan and the Inspector of Flames in al Nahud'. On a more practical level, 'Ali Dinar garrisoned the frontier hills where the Anglo–Egyptian authorities feared that his men might damage this area'[s] strange *tebeldi* trees. These were a vital source o[f] water not only for the local inhabitants but also for any army who would have to use the hills as a staging post.

Despite his colourful letter-writing style 'Al[i] Dinar was now clearly having doubts. No help had arrived from the far-away Ottomans or Sanussi. Yet once the Anglo–Egyptian attack came, 'Ali Dinar's strategy was good. He correctly judged his enemy's

ne of advance, drew them as far as possible from
heir sources of supply, and then attempted a
lanking attack as they marched past. The Fur
rmy was, in fact, defeated not by poor strategy but
y the enemy's overwhelmingly superior firepower,
vhich was now even more pronounced than it had
een during the battle of Omdurman 18 years
arlier. Three *arba'* divisions, about 3,600 men,
ought in this 40 minute battle of Beringia, with
ome 800 cavalry who never entered the battle as
heir tactical rôle was to destroy a beaten foe. More
han 250 died, including Ramadan 'Ali the
ommander and Sulayman 'Ali, an African slave
vho was second-in-command.

Back in his capital 'Ali Dinar still had his
odyguard of *kashkangiya* 'blunderbuss-men', a few
ther regulars, palace attendants, boys in military
raining and fugitives from Beringia. With these he
oped to make a stand; but the following day 'Ali
)inar's remaining men were bombed by a BE2
ircraft of the Royal Flying Corps. This further
lemonstration of the foe's technical superiority
inally broke Fur morale; the army dispersed and
Ali Dinar fled with a few faithful followers. In
)ctober one of the Sultan's sons, Zakariyah,
gathered 120 riflemen and 1,000 spear-armed
rregulars at Dibbis, but was quickly routed by
Sudanese troops of the Egyptian Army, 'Ali Dinar
imself being tracked down and killed on 6
November.

The Arab Revolt
and its Rivals

Whereas the Sanussi struggled against relatively
recent European attempts to conquer Muslim
lands, the Arab Revolt was directed against the
Muslim Ottoman Empire which had ruled most of
the Middle East for centuries. The Revolt also
began at the very heart of the Muslim world: in the
Hijaz with its holiest of Muslim cities, Mecca and
Medina. Yet the seeds of this essentially nationalist
rising had been sown in the north. Here, in Syria,
Palestine, Lebanon and Iraq, anti-Ottoman secret
societies had grown up among the educated Arab
élite of Damascus, Beirut, Baghdad and elsewhere.

The traditional Ottoman Empire was a state in
which personal identity was on the basis of religion,
where the Ottomans could boast a degree of
toleration far in advance of anything in Europe.
During the 19th and early 20th centuries the
Ottoman state had lost virtually all its European
provinces to a wave of remarkably intolerant and
racist Balkan nationalism. Not surprisingly this
stimulated a feeling of Turkish national identity
within what remained of the Empire, which
culminated in the Young Turk Revolution shortly
before the Great War.

This upheaval brought the Ottomans into line
with many aspects of European thinking, and it
concluded with the establishment of a Turkish
Republic once the Great War was over. In the
immediate pre-war years, however, the rise of
'Turkism' hit the Arab provinces hard. A brief
honeymoon between the modern-minded Young
Turks and the Arab élite was followed by

**Tuareg nobleman of southern Libya in 1920 (Royal Geographi-
cal Society).**

'Ali ibn Hussayn, leader of the Arab Southern Army with some of his followers and a Sharifian flag (Lawrence Coll., IWM).

persecution, executions and the plotting of revolt. In Iraq the ultra-secret *Ahad* society included an estimated seven out of ten Iraqi–Ottoman army officers. In Syria the *Fatah* society included intellectuals, land-owners and senior civil servants, but was less secret and consequently suffered more when the Ottoman authorities cracked down in 1914 and 1915. Far to the south the Sharif Hussayn, head of the Hashemite clan which traditionally ruled the Holy Cities, realised that the Ottoman Empire was no longer an all-embracing Islamic state but was becoming a Turkish Empire; consequently he quietly built up the power of his own Hijazi Emirate.

The reasons why the Sharif Hussayn actually proclaimed the Revolt in 1916 are very complex. The execution of Arab nationalists in Syria, demands for action from the secret societies, Ottoman pressure on him to endorse their declaration of a *jihad* or Holy War, and, not least the approach of Ottoman reinforcements all contributed. In purely military terms the moment appeared unsuitable. British prestige was at a low ebb: paralysed along the Suez Canal, defeated in Gallipoli and Iraq, and immobile in Aden, the British did not look like attractive allies. Yet the Royal Navy and an Italian fleet in Eritrea dominated the Red Sea. This ensured the Sharif's

communications with the main British power-base in Egypt, as well as a continued supply of food to the Hijaz which would otherwise have been totally dependent on the Ottomans. So the decision was made; the Arab Sharifian flag was raised, and within a short while the Sharif's followers supported by tribal volunteers, had liberated Mecca, Ta'if and the ports of Jiddah and Yanbu while the main Ottoman garrison was bottled up in Medina.

European assistance

Hussayn had hoped for a grand strategy, with a British landing in northern Syria stimulating revolt throughout Palestine, Lebanon and Syria, thus cutting Ottoman communications with her Arab provinces. But the British turned down such an ambitious plan, so the Arab Revolt was limited to the Hijaz. In its early stages the Revolt needed all the help it could get, and at first assistance came through the British-controlled Egyptian Army. An initial British advisory mission grew into an operational unit, and by the end of the war staff officers, signallers and other technicians, a squadron of armoured cars, a battery of 10-pdr. guns and a flight of RFC aircraft were a l serving with the Arab Northern Army in what is now Jordan. Generally speaking, however, the importance of this British contingent has been overstated, at least where the fighting was concerned. Its leadership was also somewhat unclear, with Col. Joyce being the senior officer while Lawrence, raised to the rank of colonel after the battle of Tafila, appeared to dominate proceedings. His precise position was

Sharifian irregulars of the Utaybah tribe at Yanbu on the Red Sea (Lawrence Coll., IWM).

Sharifian irregulars on patrol (Lawrence Coll., IWM).

unclear for, although he commanded no troops other than his bodyguard, his powerful personality ensured that he took effective control whenever tribal irregulars were involved. The ex-Ottoman officers of the Arab regular army were less impressed by a man they regarded as an archaeologist and amateur soldier, many claiming to be amused by Lawrence's sudden comings and goings, maintaining that he contributed little to operational planning. Nor, incidentally, did the Ottomans ever hear of Lawrence, let alone put a price on his head. The true value of T. E. Lawrence's rôle in the Arab Revolt will perhaps never be known, since it is now so overlaid with mythology and political axe-grinding.

The British were not alone in helping the Arab Revolt. The French also sent a force of Arab troops which, under Lt.Col. Brémond, represented the main regions of French North Africa. Their officers were Lt.Col. Cadi of the 113th Regt. of Heavy Artillery from Algeria, Capts. Raho and Sa'ad of the 2nd Algerian Spahis, and Lt. Lahlou, who commanded the Sultan of Morocco's infantry Black Guard. In October 1916 this French contingent consisted of eight machine gun sections, an artillery battery of six guns, a mountain artillery battery of six guns carried by mules, an engineer company and support personnel. A detachment of artillery and engineers under Capt. Pisani subsequently served alongside Lawrence in the Arab Northern Army. Others, including Capt. Depui who had distinguished himself at Verdun with the French Somali Bn., served with the Amir Abdullah's Southern Army in the siege of Medina, as well as with Sharif 'Ali, Sharif Hussayn, and on almost every front where the Arab armies fought. The main Arab training centre at Mecca was also staffed by French colonial officers, men from the Egyptian Army and ex-Ottoman instructors.

Nevertheless it was the Sharifian Army that bore the brunt of the Arab Revolt. Tribal irregulars formed the largest element and the Sharifian leadership knew that it was essential to win the co-operation of each tribe as the Arab armies progressed. All fighting men in the Arab forces were volunteers, ranging in age from 12 to 60 years. Among the first tribal contingents were poor mountain folk, peasants rather than nomads, who fought on foot. Warriors of bedouin origin rode camels but similarly dismounted to fight. Dressed in loose shirt-like tunic, loose cotton trousers, the traditional Arab *kafiya* headcloth and festooned with cartridge bandoliers, they came from the Bani 'Ali, Bali, Juhaynah, Utaybah and other Hijizi or west Arabian tribes. At first they were poorly armed with muzzle-loading *jazail* muskets. A few Japanese Arisaka rifles were sent by the British, but although these were excellent weapons for desert conditions the ones that arrived were old and damaged.

Though brave, these tribesmen had no military training or discipline and were generally useful only in raids or in support of smaller numbers of Arab Army regulars. Nor did the tribes all look the same, since some were wealthier or adopted subtle differences in their dress. Lawrence described the Jufa contingent as dressed in white with large red and black striped headcloths, waving palm branches instead of banners. He described the Ashraf of the Juhaynah tribe as wearing henna-dyed tunics under black cloaks, carrying swords and each having a personal slave riding on the camel's rump. British advisers were appalled by their habit of not oiling their rifles, until they also learned that oil simply attracted grit; instead the Arabs rubbed their guns clean with rags. Europeans also had to get used to their allies' habit of wearing enemy uniform after a battle, as a symbol of victory. When actually fighting, the irregulars often stripped half naked, partly to ensure clean wounds

Hamid al Manjara and other bedouin irregulars of the Sharifian Army (Lawrence Coll., IWM).

and partly to avoid damaging the few clothes they possessed.

In addition to strictly tribal forces, the Arab Army included a traditional semi-professional corps known as the Agayl. These camel-mounted mercenaries, recruited from Hijaz or Najd villagers and townsfolk, were paid in gold for a fixed period of service. Their loyalty during a contract was proverbial, but they would as happily change sides once this expired. Aged from 16 to 25, they were more amenable to discipline than the tribal irregulars, had more experience of the wider world, and were frequently extravagant in their dress, jewellery and hair-styles. Lawrence himself recruited a bodyguard of such Agayl, his men wearing every colour except white—which Lawrence reserved for himself. Though looking like 'a bed of tulips' as Lawrence himself admitted, these Agayl were loyal fighters, 60 of them being killed during the war.

The Arab Revolt also needed a hard core of trained soldiers as an example to the irregulars. Only properly disciplined troops could face the Ottomans in open battle, and these could only be recruited from Iraqi or Syrian ex-Ottoman soldiers now languishing in various POW camps. Fortunately many jumped at the chance of fighting for an Arab cause, despite the knowledge that it

Sharifian irregulars in Damascus, 1918 (Lawrence Coll., IWM).

recaptured they would be executed as traitors. Late in the summer of 1916 the British sent 1,000 such men to the Hijaz, and even at the end of the war about 90 per cent of Arab Army regulars were ex-Ottoman POWs. Armed and uniformed from British stores, they were eventually formed into two brigades, though their total strength was actually closer to one brigade. While the infantry wore British uniforms, camel and mule-riding units found these unsuitable, reverting to traditional Arab costume from the waist down. This regular Arab Army was also distinguished by its khaki *kafiya* headcloths.

In overall divisional command was the same Ja'afar al Askari who had been captured while leading Sanussi troops in the Western Desert. His brigade commanders, Nuri al Sa'id and Maulud Mukhlis, were similarly experienced ex-Ottoman officers of Iraqi origin. Most of the Arab Army's officers were, in fact, Iraqis, as were half of the other ranks. Among the Syrians and Palestinians were many who, though dedicated to Arab independence, were far from convinced by the Sharif

Hussayn's claim to leadership. Most regulars had families living in Ottoman territory, often with relatives still fighting in Ottoman ranks. Not surprisingly the Arab Army rarely wore badges of rank or anything else to help identification if killed or captured, and no unit officer was above the rank of captain. This led to a very democratic spirit but also confused the British advisors. An Ottoman background probably accounted for the presence of whisky in the officers' mess, while common military training frequently enabled Arab officers to predict their enemy's next move.

Even before Lawrence and the other British arrived, Maj. Aziz al Masri was evolving a strategic plan for the Arab Revolt. Born in Egypt of Arab and Circassian parents, he had served with the Sanussi before the war. Aziz al Masri responded immediately to the Sharif's call in 1916, becoming Hussayn's chief-of-staff and founding father of the Arab Army. His plan envisaged 8,000 Arab regulars with eight pieces of artillery and 20,000

Col. T. E. Lawrence in the uniform of the regular Arab Army (Lawrence Coll., IWM).

tribal irregulars, gradually working their way up the railway from the Hijaz through Syria to what is now the Turkish frontier. They would avoid direct confrontations with the enemy but, by constantly cutting the railway, they would bleed the Ottoman garrisons to death. This, of course, was the plan ultimately followed by the Arab Northern Army.

Late in 1916 the Sharifian Arab Army was reorganised on a territorial basis. A Northern Army based at Yanbu under the Amir Faisal had one infantry brigade, a Sharifian volunteer contingent, four artillery batteries and various tribal irregulars with which to march up the Hijaz railway and eventually take Damascus. A Southern Army at Rabigh under the Amir 'Ali had two infantry battalions, one mule battalion, one camel battalion, four artillery batteries, one engineer company and tribal contingents. This was to contain a large Ottoman garrison at Medina (which did not surrender until 1919) and watch Ottoman forces further south in Asir and Yemen. An Eastern Army at Wadi Ais under the Amir Abdullah had two camel battalions, one cavalry squadron, one mountain artillery battery, a Hashemite volunteer contingent and tribal irregulars. This kept up pressure on the powerful pro-Ottoman Shammar tribe led by Ibn Rashid in central Arabia, and stopped Ottoman supplies reaching this area, while also keeping an eye on the theoretically allied but far from friendly forces of Ibn Sa'ud (see below).

In addition to Ottoman mountain guns captured at Ta'if, some obsolete artillery arrived from the Egyptian army late in 1916, though mostly lacking sights, range-finders, range-tables and high explosive shells. (In fact the Arab Army never got sufficient artillery.) Even more vital were large numbers of Hotchkiss and Lewis light machine guns. In the high-speed raiding of the Northern Army these were snipers' tools, their users generally having neither the time nor the expertise to repair damaged weapons.

The Arab forces were the most mobile in the Middle East: by the end of the campaign the Northern Army had fought over 1,600 rail-kilometres, 4,800 camel-kilometres from Medina to Muslimiya Junction on the Turkish–Syrian frontier. On the other hand some of the distances and times claimed by Lawrence have recently been proved impossible by a British Army re-enactment

Mule-riding regular infantry of the Arab Army at Yanbu, January 1917 (Lawrence Coll., IWM).

team—a fact long recognised by Arab writers.

Within a short time the British Command in Cairo was surprised to discover that more Ottoman troops were engaged against the Arab Revolt than were facing them across the Suez Canal, and they finally started to provide more generous supplies. These were certainly needed, for the Ottomans had also realised that the Arab Revolt posed a serious threat. The Arab irregulars were, in fact, severely shaken by being unexpectedly bombed by Ottoman aircraft late in 1916. The rôle of the tiny Ottoman Air Force has never been recognised outside Turkey, and the rapid shipment of three Pfalz AIIs from the Caucasus front to the blistering heat of the Hijaz was an achievement in itself. British and French aircraft had long been active over the Red Sea, but this sudden activity by the under-rated Ottoman Air Force led to four BE2 aircraft of the Royal Flying Corps being attached to the Arab Army. To these were soon added Rolls Royce and Talbot armoured cars.

By the summer of 1917 the effectiveness of the Arab Army had improved to such a degree that Gen. Liman von Sanders was urging the Ottomans to evacuate the Hijaz entirely; but to abandon the holy cities of Mecca and Medina was politically unthinkable, so the Arab Revolt remained a bleeding wound for the Ottoman Army. Yet the Arab Army, already short of machine guns and artillery, also had its share of problems. Medical services were virtually non-existent, and it was common for men to kill severely wounded comrades rather than let them fall into enemy hands. Yet morale remained high, even in the harsh winter of 1917–18, when the Northern Army suffered 50 per cent casualties from exposure and frostbite in the highlands of south Jordan. (The British would only supply summer kit in the 'tropical' Middle East.)

The Northern Army had now reached that mosaic of religions and cultures known as Bilad al Sham, or Greater Syria. Among the first minorities to be met in the mountains were Christian Arabs, who were not merely pro-Allied but were prepared to join the Arab Army. A few Armenian families who had taken refuge around Tafila also lent their aid, though Sanussi refugees who had settled in the area were naturally more loyal to the Ottomans. For a while the Muslim Arabs of Tafila fired on the Arab Army; but the more normal pattern was for Syrian and Armenian Ottoman soldiers to change sides in large numbers, being given the Arab Army's typical khaki *kafiya* but often retaining their Ottoman uniforms and weapons. The Druze tribes who inhabited the mountains south of Damascus only joined the Arab cause in the closing stages of the campaign, but the people of Salt in central Jordan attacked the Ottoman rear even before the Arab Army had reached their town. Most of the Sunni Arab villagers of the Hauran, a broad and fertile area in what is now northern Jordan and southern Syria, declared in favour of the Revolt. Some, in their eagerness, seized weapons from the retreating Ottoman troops slightly too soon, and as a result suffered an appalling massacre at the village of Tafas. By the time the Arab Northern Army

Mustafa Effendi, an ex-Ottoman officer at the head of Arab Army regular infantry at Aqaba (Lawrence Coll., IWM).

Regulars of the Arab Army Camel Corps at Aqaba (Lawrence Coll., IWM).

entered Damascus the city was teeming with irregulars, local villagers and city-folk who had rallied to the Revolt.

The final march on Damascus became, in effect, a successful race against British troops who had broken through the Ottoman front in Palestine. The Arab Northern Army, from its base in the isolated oasis of Azraq, prepared a mobile column for the final push across 120km of desert and cultivated land via Dera'a to Damascus. This consisted of a regular contingent of 500 camel-mounted infantry under Nuri Sa'id, an Arab field ambulance, Lawrence's bodyguard of Agayl, a platoon of Gurkhas, 32 light and heavy machine guns from the British Indian Army, the French mountain artillery battery and machine guns under Capt. Pisani, a company of the Egyptian Camel Corps under Capt. Peake, three armoured cars, and two RFC aircraft. Accompanying the regulars were up to 3,000 bedouin volunteers under Sharif Nasir ibn 'Ali, Nuri al Sha'alan and the redoubtable Auda Abu Tayyi.

The triumphal entry of the Amir Faisal into Damascus on 3 October 1918, two days after the Northern Army reached the Syrian capital and one day after the British had done so, did not end the Arab Revolt. A last skirmish was fought outside Muslimiya less than a week before an armistice was signed, but by this time tensions were already mounting between the Sharif Hussayn, Britain and France. Hussayn had been declared King of the Hijaz, while the Amir Faisal hoped to be accepted as King of Greater Syria: this, however, ran counter to French and British plans and at the war's end Faisal was merely recognised as commander of a small Arab Army. Even the Arab Army's status was unclear: its members and leadership were technically still Ottoman subjects, and rebels at that. In December 1918 the Arab administration, which still controlled Damascus, asked Britain to recognise the existence of a regular Arab Army of three brigades and a gendarmerie of 28,000 men. Gen. Allenby recommended two brigades and 9,500 gendarmes, to be equipped from surplus British supplies following British demobilisation. But the British War Office referred only to the 'so-called regular Arab Army'. This was regarded as an insult, and to make matters worse the agreed supplies of surplus arms were blocked by London. Loss of confidence in British intentions grew among the Arab peoples of the Middle East, gradually developing into a wave of anti-British feeling. The rest is history.

Ibn Rashid and the Shammar

It would be wrong to think that the Arab Revolt led by Sharif Hussayn involved a rebellion against Ottoman rule throughout Arabia. Many tribes remained loyal to the Ottomans, while others were neutral. Outside Yemen the most devoted followers of the Ottomans were the Shammar tribe under Ibn Rashid, who was based at Ha'il in north-central Arabia. Ibn Rashid's family had long quarrelled with the Sharifians of the Hijaz. The Shammar had also lost control of the Najd area of central Arabia to the rising power of Ibn Sa'ud, and had fallen back on a close alliance with the Ottoman authorities. Shortly before the war the Ottomans supplied the Shammar with 12,000 rifles and a great deal of money, hoping thus to counterbalance Sa'udi power.

By 1917 Ibn Rashid still had over a thousand well-armed tribesmen under his command, plenty of ammunition and five small artillery pieces to defend Ha'il, whose walls were also in good repair. Though they remained largely dormant throughout the Great War, the Shammar exerted an influence on various campaigns simply by existing. Nevertheless Ibn Rashid suffered a significant setback at the hands of the Sharifians when, in April 1917, a complete Ottoman supply convoy was captured by the Arab Eastern Army. This led to friction between Shammar and Ottomans, as the latter refused further supplies until Ibn Rashid could guarantee the route. The Arab Eastern Army

kept up their pressure throughout 1917, and by 1918 the Shammar posed less of a threat as the Ottoman Armies were clearly in retreat. Ibn Rashid continued to dominate Ha'il after the war until, in 1919, a final clash with Ibn Sa'ud marked the end of Shammar power.

Ibn Sa'ud and the Wahhabis

Unrecognised by almost everyone outside the immediate area, another power was rising in Arabia, a power which would eventually dominate the Arabian peninsula and become a world force in its own right—Saudi Arabia. The Sa'udi kingdom, whose foundations were laid just before the Great War, was, in fact, the third state to be built by the puritanical Wahhabi sect under the leadership of the Sa'udi family. In July 1913 the Ottoman and

Qatrana station on the strategic Hijaz Railway in southern Jordan, photographed by the German Air Service in 1918 (Royal Geographical Centre, Amman).

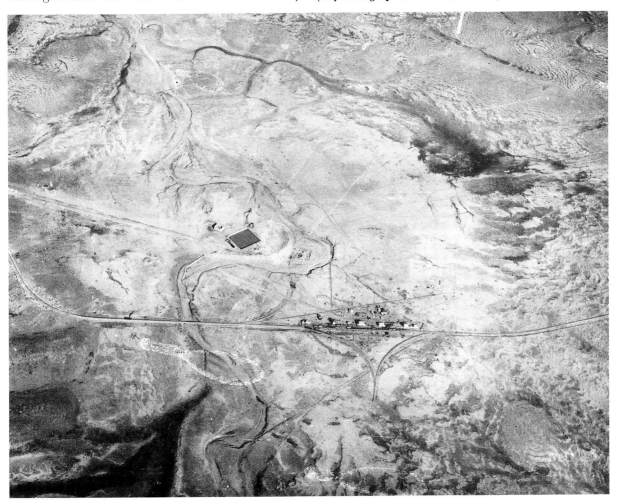

Mule-mounted machine gun section of the regular Arab Army at Aqaba (Lawrence Coll., IWM).

British Empires divided Arabia into spheres of influence on either side of a line from Qatar in the Arabian Gulf to the Aden–Yemeni border. This left Ibn Sa'ud as an awkward vassal within the Ottoman Empire. By 1914 he controlled not only Najd in central Arabia but also the Gulf coastal province of al Hasa. Ibn Sa'ud had agreed to support the Ottomans in case of war but his position was far from clear. He was also feared and mistrusted by Ibn Rashid of the Shammar, the Sharifians in the Hijaz and the pro-British Amir of Kuwait. Meanwhile Ibn Sa'ud despised them all as decadent tools of either British or Turkish imperialism.

The Sa'udi army actually played a very small part in the Great War, keeping its power dry for the struggle to control Arabia once the war was over, but it did make a few desultory attacks on the pro-Ottoman Shammar. The first clash, at Jarrab on 24 January 1915, resulted in a severe defeat during which Capt. Shakespear, a British adviser with the Sa'udis, was killed, thus ending what might have been another 'Lawrence' story. Ibn Sa'ud and Ibn Rashid agreed to a truce, thus leaving Arab liberation to the Sharifian Arab Army of the Hijaz. Ibn Sa'ud's fanatical *ikhwan* army would actually have preferred to attack the Sharifians than the Shammar or Ottomans, while Ibn Sa'ud was himself jealous of the Arab Revolt's successes. Yet he was enough of a politician to realise the necessity of earning what little aid he received from the British and to join the winning side. Ibn Sa'ud now had 8,000 modern rifles, four machine guns and about a dozen ex-Ottoman 7-pdr. guns—albeit

without gunners. But the Shammar were fast declining as a serious military factor so he had to move quickly. In the summer of 1918 Ibn Sa'ud's *ikhwan* army invaded Shammar territory and reached the walls of Ha'il, but once again they were unable to break in. By the time the war ended in November, relations between Ibn Sa'ud and the Sharif Hussayn had reached breaking point. The first major clash came at Turaba, where the *ikhwan* were victorious. Though few realised it at the time, the future of Arabia lay with Ibn Sa'ud and not with the Sharifian Arab Army which had fought so hard against the Ottomans.

Ibn Sa'ud's army was an almost medieval force, an apparent anachronism in the early 20th century. Although the people of Riyadh and its surrounding villages had long been the most loyal supporters of the Sa'udi family, the Wahhabi *ikhwan* were the most important part of the army. This 'brotherhood' had been established a few years before the Great War as agricultural colonies or *hujar* of settled bedouin under a regime of rigorous religious asceticism. By 1912 there were some 11,000 such *ikhwan*, rising to 30,000 by 1919. In addition there were about 250,000 bedouin

Palestinian volunteer for the Sharifian Arab Army in Jerusalem, 1918. He still wears much of his previous Ottoman uniform (Lawrence Coll., IWM).

British Rolls Royce tender of the Hijaz Armoured Car Company operating with the Arab Northern Army at Aqaba. Col. Joyce is in the front seat, Cpl. Lowe by the bonnet. (Lawrence Coll., IWM).

auxiliaries. Although the agricultural aspects of the *hujar* were rarely a success, they did provide a body of dedicated warriors ready for immediate mobilisation. Men could be summoned from the ages of 15 to 70, while even children of eight or nine sometimes accompanied the armies. Their style of combat remained essentially bedouin, though the *ikhwan* were also famed for their ability to make long unexpected marches to catch their foe unawares. Most fought with small-bore Mausers, while the bedouin auxiliaries were armed with a greater variety of rifles and old *jezail* muskets. Some *ikhwan* also carried spears and daggers. There was, of course, no *ikhwan* uniform, though many men replaced the bedouin *kafiya* with a simple turban to mark their break with a nomadic past.

A small cavalry force was often stationed on either side of an army leader while most men fought on foot, though camel-mounted warriors could also act as a shock force. Flank and rear attacks were used, but an assault was normally made at once, in force and without plans for withdrawal. Great emphasis was, however, placed on reconnaissance, the use of spies, speed of manoeuvre and surprise. The existence of *ikhwan* sympathisers and even members of the movement within an enemy camp naturally gave Ibn Sa'ud a considerable intelligence advantage, while the ferocity of the *ikhwan*, though not mirroring medieval Islamic practice, did tend to demoralise a foe. All enemy males, of whatever age, were normally slaughtered, while the *ikhwan* also had the un-Arab reputation of killing women and children if they overran an enemy encampment. In the event such habits led to their downfall and disbandment by Ibn Sa'ud after the war was over.

The War in Southern Arabia

The struggle between the British and Ottoman Empires around Aden is one of the most obscure episodes of the Great War. Even less is known about the actions of local peoples on this little-known front. They had, of course, been long renowned as mercenaries, many Yemenis having served in the Italian armies of Eritrea across the Red Sea. With their turbans, long brightly coloured shawls and sleeveless sheepskin winter cloaks, the people of Yemen looked very different from the northern Arabs of Saudi Arabia, Jordan, Syria and Iraq.

There had been many anti-Ottoman risings in Yemen, but by 1914 Ottoman rule seems to have been accepted, partly as a result of a recent compromise which left the Shi'ite Imam of Yemen holding religious sway in the highlands while the Ottomans carried out the mundane business of everyday government. When war broke out in 1914 the Ottomans determined to hold Yemen, as its loss would almost certainly lead to further disaffection

Arab regulars around an RFC BE2 aircraft forced down near Muzayrib in southern Syria on 17 September 1918 (Lawrence Coll., IWM).

in the holy cities of the Hijaz. A redoubtable Circassian officer, 'Ali Sa'id Pasha, defended the area with 14,000 mostly Syrian soldiers of the 7th Yemen Army Corps, two-thirds of whom were tied down in garrison duty.

A British naval bombardment of Ottoman positions in Yemeni territory at the southern entrance to the Red Sea in November 1914 further alienated the Imam of Yemen. It also angered the British–Indian authorities in Aden by undermining their efforts to win friends among the Sunni Muslim population of the coast, many of whom resented the power of the Shi'ite Imam. There was also a rival family claiming the Imamate in the mountains. In 1914, however, the Aden authorities expected no trouble from the Ottomans and were taken completely by surprise when 'Ali Sa'id Pasha went on to the offensive.

Fortunately for the British, the forces in Yemen were isolated from the rest of the Ottoman Empire after the Arab Revolt erupted in 1916. Nevertheless, without reinforcements, supplies or even regular communication from Istanbul, 'Ali Sa'id Pasha not only kept the British penned in Aden but spread Ottoman influence east into the Hadramawt and south into the Horn of Africa. Yet the Pasha was not entirely isolated; 40 German sailors from ships interned at Massawa before Italy entered the war made their way to Yemen, as did some survivors from the German raider *Emden* who reached Hudaydah in a series of commandeered

ships after being stranded in the East Indies. None, however, appear to have taken part in the fighting around Aden.

The hinterland or Protectorate of Aden had not been given much attention until there was a sudden rush by both Ottoman and British–Indian authorities to 'collect' the allegiance of various frontier tribes shortly before the Great War. Meanwhile the defence of Aden itself fell to a British garrison supported by the tiny Aden Troop, which consisted of Indian soldiers and locally recruited guides. Defence of the Protectorate depended on the local sultans and their tribal armies. Once the danger became apparent an Aden Field Force was hurriedly organised from the available Imperial troops, and by 1916 this consisted of six battalions of infantry, two squadrons of cavalry, a company of sappers and some almost obsolete artillery.

The nearest of the Protectorate leaders to Aden was the Sultan of Lahij, and in 1914 he was given rifles, ammunition and money to recruit Awlaqi tribal mercenaries just in case something flared up. The Sultan was also left responsible for gathering intelligence on Ottoman activities and for maintaining good relations with the Imam of Yemen. On paper the Sultan of Lahij seemed to have a formidable following. Like most Sultanate armies this force consisted of *asakir* feudal retainers wearing multi-coloured turbans and kilts, and armed with Martini rifles. He also employed a renegade Turkish gunner for his two Crimean War vintage muzzle-loading cannon. Next came the Sultan's *abid* or slaves, a very faithful body of men armed and dressed like the feudal *asakir* though not wearing the

The Sanussi Revolt:
1: Sayyid Ahmad al Sharif al Sanussi
2: Libyan irregular
3: Muhafiziya, Sanussi regulars

A

Revolt in the Sahara:
1: Bushir Musa of Darfur
2: Tuareg nobleman
3: Trooper, Egyptian Cavalry

B

Arabs in Ottoman service:
1: Trooper, Ottoman Cavalry
2: Druze auxiliary
3: Iraqi irregular horseman

C

The Arab Revolt:
1: Auda Abu Tayyi
2: Agayl bodyguard
3: Col. T.E. Lawrence

D

1: Ashraf irregular with slave
2: Mounted Infantryman, Sharifian Army
3: Infantryman, Sharifian Army

Yemen and the Gulf:
1: Yemeni highland auxiliary
2: Awlaqi tribal warrior
3: Lur irregular horseman

F

The Egyptian Army:
1: Sinai Gendarmerie
2: Sergeant, Camel Corps
3: Corporal, 1st Bn., Egyptian Infantry

G

Italian Colonial Troops:
1: Libyan Carabinieri
2: NCO, VII Eritrean Ascari Bn.
3: Sergeant, Agordat Camel Corps

H

ong curved dagger which was the badge of a free man. Militarily more important than both these groups were the tribesmen, who included a levy from the ruler's own tribe plus mercenaries recruited from outside. Such armies had no uniforms but wore traditional costume similar to that of the Yemen. There were, however, differences between the dress of the highlands, with its heavy sheepskins, and that of the lower regions of the Protectorate where some men wore little more than indigo-blue kilts. Local blacksmiths also made daggers, sword blades and, until recently, matchlock muskets.

Among the most warlike tribes was the Yafa, which had long sent mercenaries all around the Indian Ocean, even as far as Indonesia. The Lower Awlaqi were similarly famed as mercenaries. But all that united these bickering tribes was their cult of *kabyala*, a code of warrior ethics and local loyalties which virtually guaranteed constant feuds. Their style of warfare was that of the guerrilla, while those caught in ambushes would use their camel saddles as rudimentary field fortification. In such skirmishes women brought water to the combatants while small boys might carry a warrior's musket, powder horn and bullet pouch. Other traditional weapons included the *jimbiyah* short slashing sword; the *khanjar* dagger, smaller and more decorated but otherwise similar; the short spear with a long blade of such soft steel that it often had to be straightened after a single blow; a cavalry spear with a shorter blade; and a sling made of the stripped leaves of the aloe. This could also serve as a match for the matchlock musket. The introduction of modern firearms (of which the large-calibre 1874 Le Gras single-shot breech-loading rifle was the most popular) was already changing the pattern of warfare by 1914.

Shortly after New Year 1915 the Imam of Yemen reacted to the British shelling of Sheikh Sa'id by raiding the Protectorate frontier, and in the spring Ottoman troops seized a range of hills. Still the Aden authorities expected nothing worse, and seriously considered sending some of Aden's garrison to Somaliland, where the so-called 'Mad Mullah' had again become a threat. Meanwhile the Sultan of Lahij disbanded many of his mercenaries. The tribes were astonished by this British inactivity, while 'Ali Sa'id Pasha, the Ottoman commander,

Capt. Ismail Abdu with NCOs and other ranks of the Arab Camel Corps in 1918 (IWM).

decided that an offensive would not only confirm Yemeni loyalty but win over others. The frontier Haushabi Sultan quietly joined him, thus enabling the Ottomans to make a surprise attack at the beginning of July with about 1,600 regular troops, 3,000 local irregulars, the Haushabi tribal army, some Somali volunteers and about 20 guns. Another frontier ruler, the Sultan of Muqbil, feigned sickness until threatened with an artillery bombardment, after which his army also joined the invaders.

The remaining Protectorate sultans were now in a dilemma. Powerless on their own, most either remained neutral or went over to the Ottomans. Only the Sultan of Lahij, as the closest to Aden, could expect British help, and so hurriedly re-enlisted 2,000 men; but they were driven out of Lahij by Ottoman artillery on 3 July. Aden rushed a small force across 50km of desert in a vain attempt to hold the town, the Sultan being accidentally killed by a British bullet in a resulting military disaster. The Sultan's mercenaries, willing to fight for Lahij but not for the British, either went over to the Ottomans or retired home. 'Ali Sa'id Pasha's army reached Sheikh Othman, from where his guns could shell Aden harbour, while the Aden authorities sent messages to Egypt announcing that 'the Turks were on the golf course'. In fact the Ottomans were soon driven out of Sheikh Othman and a new Front was established around Aden which remained largely unchanged until the end of the war.

Among the many local people who actively

helped the Ottomans were two brothers from the Awlaqi tribe who had previously served in Lahij. They gained quite a reputation for ambushing British patrols. One, named Muhammad al 'Umari, became a local legend by capturing various British and Indian troops in 1917. Al 'Umari had some cavalry under his command, but his normal tactics were a refinement of traditional warfare in which his men ambushed their foes from camouflaged rifle-pits.

Several hundred Somalis made their way from Africa to join 'Ali Sa'id Pasha's force in 1916. On the other side the Aden garrison made few serious attempts to break out, as London refused to permit major offensives. Nor was much effort made to recruit troops from those locals who did support Britain. In December 1915 a hundred residents of the village of Imad were recruited as guides under British and Indian officers. This Imad Levy later grew into an Arab Levy which began making patrols against the Ottomans in March 1918. Near the very end of the war an Arab Legion—later renamed the 1st Yemen Infantry—was also recruited from the hill tribes, but was never fully used.

Both British and Ottoman Armies permitted

Sharifian Camel Corps and Sherwood Rangers of the 14th Cavalry Brigade at Muslimiya Junction on the Turkish–Syrian frontier, scene of the last action by the Arab Army (IWM).

camel caravans to pass through their lines. These brought fresh vegetables to the besieged Aden garrison, returning with fuel, rice and sugar for the tribes, plus the occasional crate of whisky for Ottoman officers. With his very limited resources 'Ali Sa'id Pasha tried to win more friends. He built roads, bridges and even a hospital at Lahij, while proclaiming Islamic solidarity and sending silken banners to the various Protectorate sultans. The Subihi tribe tried to play its own game by attacking both sides, but was punished by the Ottomans as a result. Most of the eastern Protectorate tribes remained loyal to the British because 'Ali Sa'id Pasha was not strong enough to interfere in such distant regions, while control of the sea put the British in a better position. East of the eastern Protectorate lay the vast and largely unexplored regions of the Hadramawt where Britain's treaties with local rulers were largely meaningless. Yet even the people of this area were not isolated from the war; the Ottomans sent special agents from their consulate in the Dutch East Indies on a secret mission to win over Hadramawt sultans in 1916. Some responded but most remained pro-British throughout the war; Sir Ghalib of Makalla even offered his tiny tribal army to the British (who politely declined).

When the war ended in 1918 'Ali Sa'id Pasha refused to surrender until specific orders arrived

Sketch of an Iraqi 'Budhoo' tribal irregular by Pte. Baggott of the King's Hussars (Lancs. County & Regimental Mus., Preston).

Another sketch from Pte. Baggott's notebook is said to illustrate B Squadron of the King's Hussars watching Kurdish levies punishing tribesmen who had interfered with a British surveying party. However, the Levies wear Arab costume while their victims are dressed as Kurds or Lurs (Lancs. County & Regimental Mus., Preston).

...rom Istanbul, and even then he entered Aden to a ...ero's welcome at the head of 2,655 Ottoman ...roops, 221 local irregulars and 159 women and ...hildren. Some of his men later chose to remain in ...emen, serving the now independent Imam for ...any years.

The Idrisis of Asir

...he coastal province of Asir lies south of the Hijaz in ...hat is now Saudi Arabia. Like Yemen it consists of ... coastal plain and a relatively well-watered ...ountainous hinterland. In 1914 a religious leader ...amed Sayyid Muhammad al Idrisi, having earlier ...hallenged Ottoman control, still dominated much ...f Asir. Though now closely watched by the 21st ...sir Division of the Ottoman Army, al Idrisi ...aintained links with the Italians in Eritrea and ...reatened to cut Ottoman communications with ...emen. The Sayyid further claimed not only the ...ntire Asir but also the coastal plain of Yemen. Thus ...here was every chance of him supporting the ...ttomans' external enemies in the event of war.

In fact Sayyid al Idrisi became the first Arab ruler to raise the standard of revolt during the Great War. He seized the Farasan Islands in January 1915, then signed a treaty with Britain, to whom he handed these islands. British concern about the spread of French or Italian influence in the Red Sea meant that al Idrisi was prohibited from receiving military supplies from anyone except Britain, and partly as a result of this limitation the revolt in Asir never gathered momentum. Nevertheless the Idrisis did receive rifles, ammunition, four 5-in. howitzers and 30 15-pdr. field guns, and sent gunners to Aden for training. British artillery was, however, never as popular as the rugged old field guns given to the Idrisis by Italy in 1911. In November 1915 Sayyid al Idris reached a truce with the Imam of Yemen and, with British naval support, attacked Luhayyah. Not until 1917, and again with naval support, were Idrisi forces able to capture this port, and their main contribution to the Allied war effort was, in fact, to tie down an Ottoman division and to win over many of the latter's Yemeni irregulars.

Elsewhere in the southern Red Sea the British also occupied the Kamaran and other islands in 1915, thereafter maintaining a naval blockade which ruined small coastal towns not already under Idrisi control. In desperation the Zaraniq tribes around Hudaydah volunteered to sell their ports to Britain in return for rifles with which to fight the Ottomans. This offer was, however, turned down. Instead a peculiar little naval war developed between shallow-draught *dhows* which, sailing within the coastal reefs and generally operating at night, sought to evade the British patrols. This struggle not only undermined latent pro-British feelings along the coast but enabled the Ottomans to smuggle food from Somalia. Not until the Royal Navy brought in armed coastal trawlers was the activity of these lightly armed *dhows* halted.

Iraq and the Gulf

The relatively densely populated southern regions of Iraq between Baghdad and Basra had been the most disturbed of the Ottoman Empire's Arab provinces even before war broke out. Unlike the majority of Arabs, most of the people were Shi'a rather than Sunni Muslims. These so-called Marsh Arabs, inhabiting a vast area of shifting reed-beds, islands and channels along the lower reaches of the Tigris and Euphrates rivers, were also somewhat despised by their bedouin neighbours in the surrounding semi-desert. Local loyalties were also very mixed. The bedouin Muntafiq tribe west of the rivers were traditionally loyal to the Ottoman Empire, while those east of the rivers in Iranian territory were either neutral or similarly leaned towards the Ottomans. Only among the Zubayr around Basra, in Kuwait to the west and Ahwaz (Arabistan) to the east, could pro-British sentiment be found, and even this merely reflected a need to maintain good commercial relations with India.

In November 1914 a British force captured Basra and the Faw peninsula, but Britain subsequently refused to make a clear declaration in support of local independence, thus turning friendly neutrality into widespread hostility. As a result the invading troops soon found themselves being sniped at by local tribesmen and, more worryingly, having their supplies pilfered at an alarming rate. This sniping was almost ritualistic, starting just before sunset with war-cries, drumming and a war-dance near a British outpost—a performance which the British troops came to call 'Salvation Army Meetings'. A star-shell would then be fired, and the tribesmen would disperse in preparation for firing a variety of weapons ranging from Mausers and Martini-Henrys to a large-bore *jazail* musket (operated by an individual widely known as Blunderbuss Bill). The tribesmen also became expert at penetrating the defences put around supply dumps; they were even known to crawl beneath the wire and tie the legs and muzzle of a cavalry horse before dragging it back under the wire. Poverty and starvation reached such a degree in 1915–16 that pillagers were even found to have exhumed the dead for the sake of their boots.

In 1914 oil was already important to the Allied war effort, and one of Britain's main sources of supply was Arabistan in south-western Iran. This area was ruled by the autonomous Sheikh of Muhamaria, but his relationship with Britain was resented even by his own followers. Many responded to an Ottoman call for a *jihad* during an Ottoman attempt to eject the British early in 1915. This operation, involving about six battalions of largely Iraqi–Arab troops, two cavalry regiments and about 5,000 tribal irregulars, almost succeeded. British hopes that the Sheikh of Muhamaria's own

Recruits for the Iraqi *shabana* Mounted Police in 1918. The weapon appears to be the ancient Snider carbine (IWM).

36

men could defend the pipeline were dashed, and many sections were blown up. British and Indian troops who rushed to defend the oil installations were mauled by irregulars and suffered heavy casualties before this Ottoman strike into Arabistan was beaten back.

The Ottomans next assembled 6,000 largely Iraqi infantry and cavalry under Lt.Col. Sulayman Askari, plus about 12,000 Arab and Kurdish irregulars. The Arabs had little love for their Ottoman overlords but as yet felt even less sympathy for the British invaders. From 11 to 13 April this force made an all-out attack on the British around Basra. Despite heavy British losses, which included the defeat of a squadron of the 7th Hariana Lancers by a group of Arab irregulars, the assault failed; and as the Ottomans withdrew their Arab irregulars turned upon them. Their retreat became a rout. Sulayman Askari killed himself, and never again were Ottoman regular troops able to co-operate fully with the local tribes. Generally, however, the tribes were a greater threat to Britain, and in fact British soldiers came to distrust the people of Iraq to a degree seen nowhere else in the Great War.

One group of irregulars pushed back a British thrust towards Nasiriyah by attacking them in the rear on the night of 13–14 July 1915. This whole area was a confusion of small warlike tribes inhabiting a maze of canals, marshes and open land, who were often willing to attack both British and Ottoman troops. A clash of views also developed between British military leaders, who wanted to punish any signs of Arab enmity, and political officers who hoped to win local support. The entire campaign was in fact becoming a nightmare for the British, who had neither adequate maps to guide them nor any clear idea of which tribe would support them. Even British reprisals only demonstrated the limitations of artillery, machine guns and superior numbers in the difficult marshlands, and not until the end of 1916 did clashes cease. Even so there were still large numbers of irregular Arab cavalry on the flanks of the Ottoman army at the battle of Ctesiphon. Their presence enabled the Ottomans to outflank the advancing British on 22 November 1915, forcing them to retreat to Kut, where began one of the most tragic sieges in Britain's military history. Perhaps

An Iraqi Arab arrested in the war zone accounts for himself to the crew of a British Rolls Royce armoured car and their Ottoman prisoner (IWM).

surprisingly, the beleaguered British recruited local Arab policemen, who seem to have served loyally until Kut fell.

For the rest of 1915 and 1916 British supply columns remained vulnerable to attack by irregulars who now operated both as independent bandits and as raiders on behalf of the Ottomans. Such irregulars were known to British troops as 'Budhoos'. After the fall of Baghdad on 11 March 1917, however, the attitude of many Iraqi tribes changed: it was now clear that the Ottoman Empire would lose the war. Britain also started making serious efforts to win local support, although a declaration was still not made in favour of Arab independence. Gen. Marshal, the new British commander, was keen on encouraging the Arabs to attack his enemy's communications. Yet the front line still divided the territory of the powerful Shammar Jarba', and although some tribesmen began harrying the retreating enemy in 1918 this

Lur irregulars from south-western Iran, September 1917 (IWM).

tribe remained largely loyal to the Ottomans until the very end of the war.

More effective from a British point of view were the *shabana* Arab Police who were now being recruited from western and northern tribes. A local *shabana* was set up in southern Iraq as early as 1915 to patrol the rivers against pillagers. Men were selected with the help of their own tribal leaders to be trained, uniformed and equipped along British–Indian lines. In 1916 there were still only about 400 *shabana* but by the end of the war their numbers had risen to about 2,000, mostly Arabs but with a few Kurds. Officers and NCOs were drawn from former Ottoman officials and from leading tribal families. Once properly trained and equipped this *shabana* helped put an end to 'Budhoo' raiding. In this they were helped by Maj. Eadie's Muntafiq Scouts, a bedouin levy of poachers-turned-gamekeepers recruited in 1917. Towards the end of the war another para-military levy known as the Kurdish Horse was raised by Maj. Soane in the mountains around Khanaqin.

However, this rugged frontier region posed particular problems. To the south lay Luristan which, though nominally part of Iran, had been virtually independent before the war. The Lur were akin to the Kurds—warlike, and contemptuous of the native Persians. Traditionally they also provided the Iranian Army with some of its most effective cavalry. During the war most Lur remained aloof until 1917, though one of their tribes, the Bakhtiaris, did develop a close relationship with Britain. More numerous were the Kurds themselves. As Sunni Muslims the Kurds disliked the Shi'a Persians (Iranians) and throughout the war they remained loyal allies of the Ottoman Empire. Those living in Iraq and eastern Anatolia provided the Ottoman Army with its most reliable irregulars, the Milli tribe around Diyarbakir actually serving as a distinct auxiliary unit of both cavalry and foot. They took part in the Ottoman attempt to retake Basra, while Kurds also predominated in two of the Ottoman forces which fought the Russians in western Iran in 1914.

The Kurds of Iraq and Iran suffered terribly during the Russian occupation of their mountains in 1916 and 1917. The behaviour of the Russian Cossacks, who had to live entirely off the country, was much worse than that of the almost as ill-supplied Ottomans, great numbers of the Muslim Kurds and Azarbayjanis being slaughtered before the Russians withdrew following the 1917 Revolution. Inevitably, perhaps, the Muslims turned upon those local Christian communities—Armenians, Assyrians and Nestorians—whom they accused of having collaborated with the Russians. So deep was anti-Russian sentiment among the Kurds by this time that the British, as allies of Russia, found it extremely difficult to win any Kurdish co-operation; nor were they in a position to relieve the starving people of Khanaqin, nor even to control widespread banditry.

In many ways the end of the Great War in Mesopotamia was an untidy business. The British had promised to support the Christian Assyrians and Nestorians of north-western Iran and northern Iraq, but in the summer of 1918 these people were overwhelmed by a Kurdish–Turkish counter-attack, huge numbers of Christian refugees flooding south. About 2,000 were recruited into the Assyrian Levies which, in 1919, defended Mosul from the Turks. The Armistice had, in fact, left the status of this city unclear. It was still held by Ottoman troops at the end of the war and only threats of further action by the British commander forced them to leave. Britain had won the Mesopotamian campaign without making promises to any of the indigenous peoples—in stark contrast to the situation in Syria and Palestine, where she had made many contradictory promises; yet the situation was pregnant with future problems on both sides of the great Syrian Desert.

The Great War in central and eastern Iran falls outside the scope of this book, but there were other minor military actions on the southern side of the Arabian Gulf. In Doha a small and isolated Ottoman garrison was finally forced to surrender, its little fort being handed over to the Sheikh of Qatar. At the end of 1914 the British had also sent reinforcements to Muscat, Matrah and Sidib on the Arabian side of the Gulf of Oman. On 11 January 1915 their fears of a rising in response to the Ottoman *jihad* were justified when 3,000 tribesmen came down from the mountains to attack the Sultan of Oman's palace at Bayt al Falaj. There they met a line of British–Indian troops, while the Sultan's own men lined the ancient city walls. It was a brief battle, with the Omani tribesmen attacking in the darkness at 2 am, and pushing back the right of the British line, before being driven off with the loss of about 200 casualties when dawn came. Thereupon the revolt collapsed, the tribesmen went home and Muscat reverted to its normal but vital rôle as a British base-area for the remainder of the war.

The Egyptian Army

In 1914 Egypt was theoretically still part of the Ottoman Empire but was in reality under British occupation. Many Egyptians admired the recent Young Turk Revolution but the Egyptian élite was more 'Arab' in its political aspirations. Whereas the mass of the population regarded Egypt's titular ruler, the Khedive Abbas II, as a champion of Arab causes, he was seen as dangerously pro-Ottoman by the British. Abbas was, in fact, in Istanbul when war broke out and remained there after Britain had him deposed on 17 December 1914. On this date Prince Kamal al Din Hussayn was proclaimed sultan of a supposedly independent Egypt which, however, remained under tight British control. A number of supposedly pro-Ottoman Army officers were also arrested.

As early as November 1914 Britain declared that it would make no military demands upon Egypt or its army, asking merely for the country's benevolent neutrality while Britain did the fighting. Within a few days, however, the British military authorities realised that they needed the Egyptian Army after all. Egyptian artillery was rushed to support Indian units defending the Suez Canal, elements of the Egyptian Camel Corps having already been sent there in August. Next, all military reservists were recalled, while reinforcements from the Coast Guard Camel Corps were sent to the western frontier in case of trouble from the Sanussi. A detachment of Army engineers was also sent to the Canal in January 1915.

Tribesman of the Aden Protectorate with a Le Gras carbine shortly before the Great War.

In 1914 the Egyptian Army was a small but relatively well-equipped force under an officer corps which included many British volunteers. It consisted of two squadrons of cavalry, three companies of mounted infantry, six field and mountain artillery batteries, plus machine guns, three companies of garrison artillery and 17 infantry battalions. The ethnic origins of such infantry illustrated the Army's roots in 19th century Egyptian history. Eight battalions consisted of Egyptians, seven of Muslim Sudanese, one of Arab or largely bedouin Sudanese, and one of Equatorial south Sudanese. In addition there were a territorial company of Nuba Rifles from the Sudanese Nuba Mountains, and six companies of Sudanese reservists. The élite of the Egyptian Army was, however, the Camel Corps. This was recruited largely in the Sudan, though it had at least one Egyptian detachment, while the officers were Egyptian or British. Support troops included engineers, medical units and others. Though it was not strictly part of the Army, Egypt also had a paramilitary Coast Guard and various gendarmerie formations, many of which consisted of camel-mounted infantry.

Coast Guards on the Egyptian border with Ottoman-ruled Palestine were involved in skirmishes with Ottoman-led bedouin as soon as war broke out. Thereafter the Ottomans invaded the Sinai Peninsula in force, reaching the Suez Canal

but not bothering to mop up various isolated Egyptian outposts further south. Most of the troops which defended the Suez Canal in 1915 were from British or Indian units, yet Egyptians were also present. The 5th Artillery Battery rendered good service during an Ottoman attack between the Great Bitter Lake and Lake Timsah in February, subsequently being mentioned in despatches by Gen. Maxwell. To Britain's surprise the Egyptian Army did not respond to the Ottoman call for a *jihad* against the occupying British, the majority of Egyptians regarding it merely as a political stratagem. There were no attempts at sabotage and apart from a few Coast Guards, the only Muslim troops to be affected by the *jihad* were from British–Indian units.

Two hundred and sixty kilometres south of Suez, and totally isolated except by sea, a small Egyptian garrison still held the old Sinai quarantine station of al Tur. Another held the mining port of Abu Zinimah. After both were raided by bedouin, 200 reinforcements arrived from the 2nd Egyptian Bn. under a British officer, *Bimbashi* Pott. A large force of German-led bedouin then invaded al Tur while the Egyptians dug in and awaited the arrival of half a battalion of Gurkhas. The bedouin were driven back in a sudden counter-attack on 13th February. As British troops gradually pushed the Ottomans out of Sinai the Sinai Camel Police helped 'turn round' the bedouin and convert them into a vital source of information. Other Egyptian units patrolled 1,500km of Egyptian–Sudanese coastline to stop Ottoman communication with dissident

Idrisi artillerymen from Asir being trained in Aden by the 2/1st Devon Battery (IWM).

groups such as the Sanussi or 'Ali Dinar.

On 6 November 1915 the German submarine *U-35* shelled Sollum, sinking the Coast Guard cutter *Abbas*, damaging the *Nur al Bahr* (later to play a part in the Arab Revolt) and being engaged by the Egyptian artillery, which was also in action against Sanussi forces besieging Sollum. All forces were then withdrawn from these isolated desert outposts. British doubts about Egyptian loyalty were apparently confirmed when 12 officers, two officer cadets and 120 other ranks defected from the Coast Guard Camel Corps at Mersa Matruh during this withdrawal. The defectors joined the Sanussi; some took part in the battle of Jabal Madwa, where their dead were found still wearing Egyptian uniforms. One officer, Muhammad Salih, commanded Sanussi troops at Siwa oasis in 1917 but was later pardoned and rejoined the Egyptian Army.

Following withdrawal from the Western Desert some Egyptian cavalry were based at Wadi Natrun, while engineers, infantry, a newly formed machine gun section and some artillery were incorporated into Gen. Maxwell's Western Frontier Force. Described as a 'scratch lot', this mixed British, Indian and Egyptian force nevertheless contained the first Sanussi invasion while suffering quite heavy casualties. The main Egyptian rôle was to defend the Daba's railhead, while an armoured train manned by two Egyptian 12.5-pdr. guns and some Gurkhas patrolled the railway itself. The Egyptians continued to play a minor rôle against the Sanussi in 1916, the Coast Guard Camel Corps providing guides for British armoured cars during their dramatic rescue of prisoners held at Bir Hakim in Libya. A small detachment of Egyptian cavalry garrisoned Kharga oasis against Sanussi raids from neighbouring oases in March 1916. While British forces patrolled the Nile from Aswan to Wadi Halfa, Egyptian artillery manned boats which patrolled the river to the south as far as the great Nile bend. Local forces were also organised in the Sudan's Nubian provinces at a time when there was considerable fear not only of Sanussi raids but of a possible link-up between the Sanussi and 'Ali Dinar in Darfur. Further tribal forces were recruited to watch over the ancient *Darb al arba'ain* (Forty Days Road) caravan route which ran from Egypt's Kharga oasis to Darfur. Other tribes were encouraged to hold the hills around Darfur.

Recruits of the 1st Yemen Infantry photographed shortly after the Great War.

The Egyptian Army's only independent contribution to the Allied war effort was, in fact, the Darfur Campaign. Even before 'Ali Dinar, the Sultan of Darfur, declared against the Anglo–Egyptian authorities in Khartoum, the latter sent units of its Anti-Slavery Department Camel Police to watch the frontier, while the Camel Corps outposts at Nahud and Odaiya were reinforced. When the showdown finally came in March 1916 the Darfur Field Force under Lt.Col. Kelly consisted of five companies of Camel Corps, two of mounted infantry, six of black Sudanese infantry, two of Arab–Sudanese infantry, three of Egyptian infantry, plus six mountain guns, 14 machine guns (some with British crews), five transport companies with 1,200 camels, and medical and support units. The force was also accompanied by a flight of British aircraft. The real achievement of this campaign lay not so much in military success against a ferocious but primitive opposition, but in overcoming immense logistical obstacles. 'Ali Dinar's capital at al Fasher actually lay almost 1,000km from the Nile, and 450km from the nearest Egyptian military base. It is also a reflection on the prejudices of the time that a leading newspaper could write, 'it is particularly gratifying that the "Gippy" should have stood up and beaten his once most dreaded foe'. This was not the last operation in Sudan. Egyptian troops were

Sudanese infantry of the Egyptian Army beside the Nile during the Darfur Campaign, 1916.

subsequently involved in putting down various minor tribal risings, that by the 'Mek' of Jabal Miri in the southern Kordofan province being the most serious.

The rôle of Egyptian military advisers in the Arab Revolt has already been described, but Egyptian troops were also fighting in support of the Sharifian Arab Army from the earliest days. One section consisted of a mountain battery with some machine guns and four archaic Krupp field guns. Two British officers, Joyce and Davenport, later took over command of Egyptian units in Arabia, Joyce fighting alongside Lawrence with the Arab Northern Army while Davenport served with the Arab Southern Army where the Egyptian contribution was perhaps more significat. Here the war was more static than that of the wide-ranging Northern Army, where only the Camel Corps could find a useful rôle. Davenport's men were by no means inactive and conducted many night raids against Ottoman positions. Five Egyptian soldiers captured during such a raid later escaped from an ambushed train during one of the Northern Army's attacks on the Hijaz railway. In fact the solid

Egyptian infantry and artillery seem to have been among the most effective troops in the Southern Army.

The best-known Egyptian unit to fight alongside the Arab Northern Army was a Camel Corps detachment under *Bimbashi* Peake, the British officer who would later create Jordan's famous Arab Legion. Unlike most Egyptian Camel Corps units this was recruited from Egyptian *fallahin*, which probably accounted for its totally unflappable character and somewhat unbelligerent attitude when compared with the ferociously enthusiastic Arab troops. Armed with Martini-Henry rifles, the Camel Corps troops fought in a typically Egyptian manner, with caution, by the book, and with an apparently total disregard for enemy fire. In the later stages of the Arab Revolt they were converted into a sapper unit. This made better use of the Egyptians' higher standards of discipline and training, as well as their ability to remain calm under fire while demolishing a railway line and unable to shoot back. Despite unsympathetic remarks by Lawrence, the conversion of infantry into combat engineers was a compliment to their military value. Egyptian troops also served in Palestine as part of Gen. Allenby's Expeditionary Force; none, however, were in the front line.

Number 49 Balloon Section employed Egyptian infantry as ground handlers, while men of the 1st Egyptian Infantry Bn. not only guarded the port of Aqaba but also built a section of strategic motor road through the rugged Wadi Itm Pass.

The Plates

A: The Sanussi Revolt
A1: Sayyid Ahmad al Sharif al Sanussi
Sayyid Ahmad was a major figure in the Sanussi movement. Since the Sanussi were reformers but not ascetics, their leaders often wore clothes of the finest materials. Libyan traditional costume differed from Arab Middle Eastern dress, though leading personages did adopt the *kafiya* headcloth. Here it is worn beneath a white cotton cloth that served as a mark of the Sanussi family. Sayyid Ahmad also wears the old-fashioned soft red *fez* hat that had been replaced by a stiffer version in Egypt and the Ottoman Empire.

A2: Libyan irregular
The bulk of Sanussi forces consisted of Libyan tribesmen like this warrior, who wears full traditional costume including the *haik*, a long piece of heavy white woollen material wrapped around the body and over the head. His bandolier is of local manufacture, but his rifle is a captured Italian Mannlicher-Carcano Model 91 Cavaleria (cavalry) carbine with a rearward-folding bayonet. The traditional decoration on his horse's harness indicates that he is from a wealthy tribe or family.

A3: Muhafiziya of the Sanussi regular army
Ottoman-trained *Muhafiziya* formed the disciplined core of the largely irregular Sanussi army. In battle they often wore traditional dress over their uniforms, as did the Ottoman officers who led them. Here, however, a *Muhafiziya* is shown in the uniform that was still worn in 1918 after peace had been agreed. Much of his equipment is locally made but his tunic is still in the Ottoman pattern. His weapon is a captured Italian Mannlicher-Carcano Model 91 Fanteria (infantry) rifle.

B: Revolt in the Sahara
B1: Bushir Musa of Darfur
Bushir Musa led the cavalry in the Fur army during Sultan Ali Dinar's revolt. Almost no photographs survive from this brief campaign, but Bushir Musa is here based upon a detailed description dating from the battle of Beringia. The military dress of the Fur had clearly not changed since the days of the Mahdist revolt, and this is confirmed by weapons captured during the campaign, as well as by traditional harnesses and clothing still to be found in Darfur. (Much of this reconstruction is based upon ethno-archaeological research by Graham Reed.)

B2: Tuareg nobleman
The famous Tuareg of the Saharan desert were characterised by dark blue headcloths with which they covered their faces. Such costume had been known for at least a thousand years, but Tuareg styles were neither universal nor unchanging. This man is from the Tibesti Mountains in Algeria, and carries a typical northern Tuareg sword. Some warriors now had firearms, but here we show traditional javelins held in a small quiver slung from the camel saddle, plus an enormous leather shield. Tuareg males also carried a multitude of totemic objects in leather pouches.

B3: Cavalry trooper of the Egyptian Army
The crushing of 'Ali Dinar's revolt was a purely Egyptian affair. Following British occupation in

Egyptian cavalry stationed at Kharga oasis west of the Nile in March 1916 (IWM).

Troops of the Egyptian Camel Corps with the Arab Northern Army at al Wajh (IWM).

1882 the Egyptian Army was remodelled along British–Indian lines, though a few previous Ottoman military features were retained. These included colours associated with various sections of the army, such as the red and black of this trooper's lance pennon and cummerbund. He is wearing parade dress; this was unlike the ceremonial uniform, which retained even more Ottoman characteristics.

C: Arabs in Ottoman service
C1: Ottoman Arab cavalryman
A large part of the pre-war Ottoman Army was recruited from the Arab provinces and many Arabs still fought in its ranks in 1918. Their equipment was generally identical to that of men from the Turkish provinces, though there was a wider use of the *kafiya* headcloth; on the other hand many Ottoman soldiers, particularly cavalry, adopted this practical device when serving in desert areas. During the Great War Ottoman uniform varied considerably in colour and quality, while belts, pouches and buckles could be of crude manufacture. Equipment was generally rugged and practical. Note also this man's Mauser Model 1893 (Turk) rifle.

C2: Druze auxiliary
Many thousands of irregulars fought alongside the Ottoman Army against the Russians in the Caucasus and the British in Sinai, Palestine and Iraq. They were recruited from all sections of Muslim society, urban, rural and nomadic. This man wears typical Syrian rural costume, probably from the Jebel Druse villages south of Damascus. He is armed with a Circassian dagger, a privately purchased French St. Etienne 38mm revolver, and

a composite rifle in which an Italian cavalry carbine has been fitted to a German carbine stock.

C3: Iraqi 'buddho' irregular horseman
During the confused Mesopotamian campaign the majority of Iraqi bedouin tribes fought first as allies of the Ottomans and later on their own account, seeking only survival. Their armament remained traditional, although they were still extremely dangerous to both British and Ottoman troops. Bedouin costume differed very slightly from province to province, and this moderately prosperous tribesman could have come from Mosul. His blue and white sleeveless *aba* cloak has a small amount of embroidery, while his horse's harness and saddlecloth are decorated in a characteristic Iraqi manner. He is armed only with the percussion-cap musket known throughout the Middle East as a *jezail*.

D: The Arab Revolt
D1: Auda Abu Tayyi
Auda was one of the most famous Arab warriors in 1914, and his recruitment to the Sharifian cause gave a great boost to the Arab Revolt as he was also leader of the most powerful tribe in southern Jordan. Photographs mostly show Auda wearing the mixture of traditional and Westernised dress common in an area long under European influence. This included the basic long-sleeved cotton *dishdashah* beneath a sports jacket or *jaketah* and a long-sleeved *aba* coat. He carries an Arab *khanja* dagger and a French Lebel 8mm Model 1892 pistol.

D2: Agayl bodyguard with Sharifian flag
Agayl mercenaries were recruited as bodyguards by many leaders of the Arab Revolt, including T. E. Lawrence. They were noted not only for their courage but also for their love of extravagant clothing and personal ornament. Like the bedouin

many greased their plaited hair with butter. This man carries a Japanese Arisaka rifle, supplied by Britain early in the Arab Revolt; its sliding breech-cover made it particularly suitable for dusty desert conditions. The colours of the Sharifian banner still form the basis of many Arab national flags, most obviously those of Palestine and Jordan. They represented the black, green and white of the first three Islamic ruling or leading families (Abbasids, Alids and Umayyads) plus the red of the Sharifian clan which had dominated Hijaz for centuries.

D3: Col. T. E. Lawrence

'Lawrence of Arabia' is usually portrayed in Arab costume, but on many occasions he had to wear the uniform of a regular Sharifian officer, and as such he appears here. These uniforms were essentially British, while *kafiya* headcloths often seemed to reflect personal preference, at least where Lawrence was concerned. His Short Lee Enfield No. 1 Mark III rifle had been captured by the Ottomans at Gallipoli, given a gold inscription and donated to the Sharif of Mecca, who in turn gave it to Lawrence. (An illustrated article on Lawrence's Arab costumes may be found in *Military Illustrated Past and Present* magazine, No. 4, pp. 50–52.)

E1: Ashraf tribal irregular with slave-retainer

The Ashraf of Hijaz were not a tribe but a group of families claiming descent from the Prophet Muhammad. Their fighting men joined the Sharifian Revolt as a distinctive group, and mostly wore henna-dyed cotton *abas*. Though many were extremely poor, their status almost obliged them to possess slaves who were, in reality, more like personal servants, carrying their masters' firearms (here a breech-loading Snider and a more modern Martini 'Muscat' commercial rifle), while the Ashraf carried his own prestigious sabre. The slave wears the remains of an Ottoman officer's tunic, the wearing of captured clothing being a widespread symbol of victory among Arab irregulars.

E2: Mounted infantryman of the Sharifian Army

Many of the Arab Revolt's first regular mounted infantry were recruited among the Bali tribe. Some of their equipment was supplied by the British, some by the Egyptian Army. The men soon realised, however, that traditional Arab *sirwal* baggy

Egyptian Camel Corps and local tribesmen guarding the gate of al Wajh in the Hijaz (IWM).

trousers were more practical when riding mules over long distances. Although many of the Arisaka rifles issued to these first troops arrived in appalling condition, the weapon itself was very sound.

E3: Sharifian regular infantry

As the war progressed more equipment was released by the British authorities until, by 1918, the regular Sharifian army was moderately well supplied. Apart from the Arabs' khaki *kafiya* headcloth the only major difference between the combat dress of British and Sharifian troops was the latter's lack of insignia and forms of identification, since so many had families still living within Ottoman territory. The Short Lee Enfield was now standard issue, and became known among the Arabs as the Sharifian Rifle.

F: Yemen and the Gulf
F1: Yemeni highland tribal auxiliary

The fighting between British and Ottoman troops

Ground handlers of the Egyptian Army with No. 49 Balloon Section in Palestine, 1917 (IWM).

around Aden is one of the least-known episodes of the Great War. Generally speaking the northern Yemenis remained loyal to their Ottoman rulers, many fighting as auxiliaries against the British in south Yemen or against Arab rebels in Asir province. Most of these irregulars had only old firearms, such as this man's locally decorated Springfield percussion rifle. He also carries a short Yemeni sabre and the *khanjar* dagger which, with its extravagantly upturned scabbard, remains a symbol of masculinity in parts of Yemen. The rest of his attire shows how different Yemeni traditional costume was from that of central and northern Arabia.

F2: Awlaqi tribal warrior from Hadramawt
If Yemeni highlanders possessed an old-fashioned armoury, that of the tribal *asakir* or soldiers of the virtually uncharted Hadramawt was practically medieval. Their rudimentary costume, consisting basically of a kilt, stemmed directly from pre-Islamic times. Locally made *bunduq* matchlock

muskets were still widespread, though the double ended spear was now largely symbolic. Note tha the *khanjar* dagger differed from those of the Yemen highlands, having more in common with those o Oman.

F3: Lur irregular cavalry
Another of the Great War's little-known side-show was fought in Iran, and among those involved were Lur tribes from the southern Iran–Iraq frontier Akin to the Kurds, the Lur had once supplied Iran with some of its best cavalry, but during the Great War most fought simply for survival. British soldiers generally lumped them together with the Iraqi bedouin as troublesome 'buddhos'. The Lurs were, in fact, distinguished by large round felt caps and equally bulky cloaks. Many also seem to have used lever-action Martini rifles of the so-called 'Muscat' design, thousands of which had been sold throughout the Middle East.

G: The Egyptian Army
G1: Sinai Gendarmerie
Though there was very little pro-Ottoman senti-

46

ment in Egypt during the Great War, there was considerable resentment against British occupation. Britain consequently doubted the reliability of the Egyptian Army which, nevertheless, did fight in the First World War. Among those first involved was the para-military Sinai Gendarmerie which was recruited from Sinai bedouin, and officered by Egyptian regulars. Their uniform and equipment mirrored that of the Army while retaining many traditional Arab features. Short Lee Enfield rifles were issued during the course of the war.

G2: Sergeant of the Egyptian Army Camel Corps

Camel Corps troops supported the Arab Revolt from the very beginning. In those early days they were equipped with Martini Enfield rifles of late 19th-century vintage and, like other Egyptian units, wore colour-coded cummerbunds. The cotton cover worn over their traditional red *fez* caps differed from that of the infantry in having a longer neck-covering.

G3: Corporal of the 1st Battalion, Egyptian Army

The 1st Battalion was based at Aqaba in southern Jordan. By 1917 most Egyptian infantry had been re-issued with British Short Lee Enfield rifles, but their uniforms still retained the red *fez*, a cotton *fez*-cover with battalion number on the front, and the winter-issue heavy woollen sweater seen since the battle of Omdurman in 1896.

H: Italian colonial troops

H1: Libyan Carabiniere

Italy recruited many Libyan troops before and during the Great War. Generally speaking they proved very unreliable and frequently deserted to the Sanussi Revolt. The uniform of para-military Libyan Carabinieri was closely based on that of Italian cavalry, though distinguished by an overall brown colour, and the soft red *fez* as a concession to local tradition. The red cummerbund served, like those of Egyptian troops, as a clearly visible form of unit identification.

H2: NCO of the VII Eritrean Ascari Battalion

Eritrean troops formed the most loyal and effective units in the Italian colonial army even as late as the Second World War. Many fought in Libya against the Sanussi, though it is not clear whether they still

Bugle band of the 1st Infantry Battalion Egyptian Army and the Jerusalem Municipal Guard of Honour accompanying the Prophet's Banners from Jerusalem's Temple Mount to Nabi Musa on 24 April 1918 (IWM).

wore their traditional kilted white uniforms and tall *fezes*. Once again this soldier has a distinctive unit waist-sash, and is armed with a Mannlicher-Carcano Model 91 Fanteria rifle.

H3: Sciumbasi (sergeant) of the Agordat Camel Corps

Other Eritrean units included a Camel Corps recruited in the mountainous Agordat region close to the Sudanese frontier. Like most other Eritrean colonial forces, the Agordat Camel Corps remained loyal to Italy and continued to be supplied with the best available equipment, in this case a Mannlicher Carcano Model 91 Cavalleria carbine and a pistol of unknown type.

Index

Figures in **bold** refer to illustrations

COMPANION SERIES FROM OSPREY

CAMPAIGN
Concise, authoritative accounts of history's decisive military encounters. Each 96-page book contains over 90 illustrations including maps, orders of battle, colour plates, and three-dimensional battle maps.

WARRIOR
Definitive analysis of the appearance, weapons, equipment, tactics, character and conditions of service of the individual fighting man throughout history. Each 64-page book includes full-colour uniform studies in close detail, and sectional artwork of the soldier's equipment.

NEW VANGUARD
Comprehensive histories of the design, development and operational use of the world's armoured vehicles and artillery. Each 48-page book contains eight pages of full-colour artwork including a detailed cutaway.

ORDER OF BATTLE
The most detailed information ever published on the units which fought history's great battles. Each 96-page book contains comprehensive organisation diagrams supported by ultra-detailed colour maps. Each title also includes a large fold-out base map.

ELITE
Detailed information on the organisation, appearance and fighting record of the world's most famous military bodies. This series of 64-page books, each containing some 50 photographs and diagrams and 12 full-colour plates, will broaden in scope to cover personalities, significant military techniques, and other aspects of the history of warfare which demand a comprehensive illustrated treatment.

AIRCRAFT OF THE ACES
Focuses exclusively on the elite pilots of major air campaigns, and includes unique interviews with surviving aces sourced specifically for each volume. Each 96-page volume contains up to 40 specially commissioned artworks, unit listings, new scale plans and the best archival photography available.

COMBAT AIRCRAFT
Technical information from the world's leading aviation writers on the century's most significant military aircraft. Each 96-page volume contains up to 40 specially commissioned artworks, unit listings, new scale plans and the best archival photography available.